Wild Wheels

By Edward Radlauer

AN ELK GROVE BOOK

 CHILDRENS PRESS, CHICAGO

Cover photo by Dan Radlauer
Photo page 11 by Nick Tolman

Library of Congress Cataloging in Publication Data

Radlauer, Edward.
    Wild wheels.

    (Ready, get set, go books)
    SUMMARY: Photographs and simple text introduce dif-
ferent kinds of wheels used on racing vehicles.
    "An Elk Grove book."
    1. Automobiles, Racing—Juvenile literature.
2. Motorcycles—Juvenile literature. 3. Bicycles and
tricycles—Juvenile literature. 4. Wheels—Juvenile
literature. [1. Automobiles, Racing. 2. Wheels]
I. Title.
TL147.R35   629.2'48   74-8460
ISBN 0-516-07419-9

Ready, Get Set, Go Books

Ready

Motorcycle Mania
Flying Mania

Get Set

Fast, Faster, Fastest
Wild Wheels

GO

Soap Box Racing
Ready, Get Set, Whoa!

Tires and Wheels

Racing karts use small slicks.

Slicks are good for speed, but dune buggies
need sand tires. Sand tires are wide.

Dragsters need the biggest slicks.
The slicks are for speed,
and the small tires are for steering.
Speed is important, but good tires are
very important. Bad tires don't win races.

Tricycle Wheels

A tricycle has three wheels.

In a tricycle race, you see lots of tricycles.
Do you see much speed?

No. At two miles per hour,
there's not much speed in a tricycle race.
But even at two miles per hour,
it's lots of fun.

Wheels Doing Wheelies

You can pull a low wheelie on a minibike.

You can pull a high wheelie on a motorcycle.
It's a little hard to hold a motorcycle wheelie.

You can pull a high or a low wheelie
in a funny car. Going up is great.
Coming down can be hard if you lose speed.
In any wheelie, it's important not to lose speed.

Flying Wheels

Up in the sky is a place to see flying wheels.

During a race, dune buggy wheels go flying.
All it takes is a lot of speed over a jump.

Motorcycle wheels are good for flying.
Flying on a motorcycle can be great fun.
But before you try flying motorcycle wheels,
be sure you know how to land.

Small Wheels

There are small wheels on an antique model car.

A propellor car has small wheels and a propellor.

You can make your own small wheels out of wire.
Just bend the wire into the shape you want.
If you shape it and bend it right,
you have a motorcycle.

Train Wheels

Some train wheels are old enough to be antique.

An electric train can be antique, too,
but it has smaller wheels.

You can see that this train is not electric.
It's not antique either. It may be small,
but it's doing a big job.

Motorcycle Wheels

A speedway cycle has a thin wheel in front.

You can tell this isn't a speedway bike.
Are its knobbies good for racing or flying?

A drag racing motorcycle has a thin tire in front
and a wide slick in the back.
A wide slick is good for fast starts and speed.
That's what drag racing is all about.

Antique Wheels

An antique fire engine needs antique wheels.

Does an antique car need an antique driver
or just a driver in an antique dress?

Not all antique cars have antique engines.
This 1932 Chevy may look like an antique,
but it has a racing engine.

Chopper Wheels

A chopper bicycle has an extended fork.

To be a chopper, a tricycle needs
an extended fork and a low frame.

A three-wheel, super-custom chopper needs
a long and low frame. The cover in the back
will keep the sun off your head.

Minibike Wheels

Some minibike wheels are strong and heavy.

Other minibike wheels are not so strong.
They're more for show than go.

A very long, very low minibike may not
be very heavy. This model is good
for show and it has lots of go.

Truck Wheels

Sometimes a truck can be a house, too.

Now that's wild! A bird on a cement truck.
That's one way for a bird to go round and round.

is isn't a cement truck.

s a chicken pox truck.

a chicken pox truck wilder

an a bird on a cement truck?

Racing Wheels

Quarter midget wheels can go 40 miles per hour.

Sport car wheels are faster than quarter midget wheels. They'll go over 100 miles per hour.

Gran Prix car wheels are fastest.
Gran Prix wheels may go over 150 miles per hour.
That's faster than quarter midget wheels
or sport car wheels.

Custom Wheels

You see custom wheels on a super-custom car.

A chopper uses custom wheels, too.
Super-custom wheels make a super-custom chopper.

The Green Pepper has more than custom wheels.
It has a custom Santa Claus.
Would you like Santa Claus to leave
the Green Pepper at your house?

Wild Wheels

A Bugs Bunny and friends car is kind of wild.

Wild is right! If you want your feet to feel wild,
try sliding behind your motorcycle.

When wheels get the wildest, watch out.
Watch out while a rider slides down a hill
with his motorcycle sliding behind him.
That has to be the wildest wheels.

Where to find . . .